NATIONAL GEOGRAPHIC KiDS

weird but true!

GROSS

NATIONAL GEOGRAPHIC
WASHINGTON, D.C.

HOUSEFLIES VOMIT DIGESTIVE JUICES ONTO THEIR FOOD, WHICH LIQUEFY THEIR MEALS SO THEY CAN SUCK THEM UP.

BY AGE **70,** THE AVERAGE PERSON HAS **SHED 105** POUNDS (48 KG) **OF SKIN.**

A BUS IN THE U.K. IS POWERED BY WASTE GASES FROM HUMAN POOP AND ROTTING FOOD SCRAPS.

GROSS

THAT'S GROSS!

RHINOS POOP IN PILES THAT ARE

6

TALLER THAN A TWO-YEAR-OLD.

THE GERMIEST PLACES IN A HOTEL ROOM? LIGHT SWITCHES AND TV REMOTES,

ACCORDING TO ONE STUDY.

THE U.S. FOOD AND DRUG ADMINISTRATION ALLOWS UP TO **19 MAGGOTS** AND **74 MITES** IN A SMALL CAN OF MUSHROOMS.

A COLLEGE FOOTBALL PLAYER **THREW UP** ON THE BALL DURING A CHAMPIONSHIP GAME—AND THEN SNAPPED IT TO THE QUARTERBACK.

IN CHINA, YOU CAN SIP **TEA MADE** FROM LEAVES **FERTILIZED** BY PANDA POOP.

NO, THANKS.

A FLOCK OF 50 CANADA GEESE CAN PRODUCE **5,000 POUNDS** (2,268 kg) OF POOP EACH YEAR

—ABOUT THE SAME WEIGHT AS
SIX GRAND PIANOS!

A group of girls in Nigeria developed a **pee-powered generator** that can provide **six hours of power on one quart (.95 L) of urine.**

THE MAIN INGREDIENT IN BIRD'S NEST SOUP, A COMMON DISH IN SOUTHEAST ASIA, IS **BIRD SPIT.**

13

Dried **frog guts** are a delicacy in China.

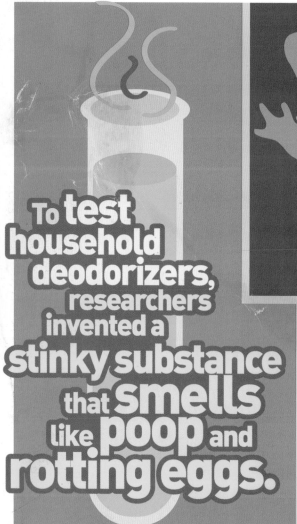

To **test household deodorizers,** researchers invented a **stinky substance** that **smells** like **poop** and **rotting eggs.**

Head lice can crawl at a speed of about nine inches (23 cm) **per minute.**

Your **heart** creates enough pressure to **squirt** **blood** up to **30 feet.**

(9 m)

Your **nose** makes a fresh batch of **mucus** every **20 minutes.**

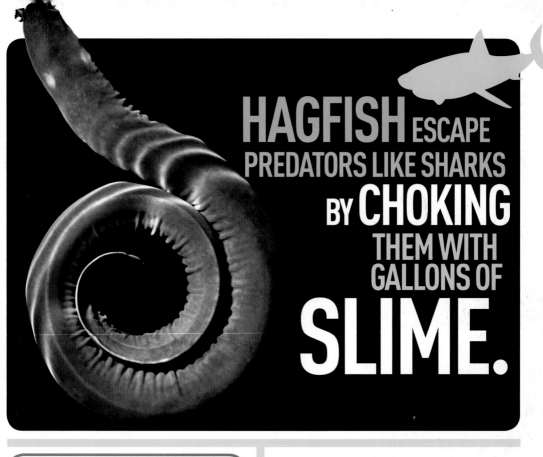

HAGFISH ESCAPE PREDATORS LIKE SHARKS BY **CHOKING** THEM WITH GALLONS OF **SLIME.**

Crocodiles can digest **bones** and horns.

Manatees use their toots to move up and down in the water.

BURROWING OWLS COLLECT ANIMAL DROPPINGS AND USE THEM AS BAIT TO ATTRACT ONE OF THEIR FAVORITE SNACKS: POOP-SEEKING DUNG BEETLES.

UH-OH ...

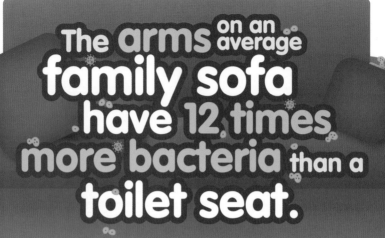

The **arms** on an average **family sofa** have 12 times more **bacteria** than a **toilet seat**.

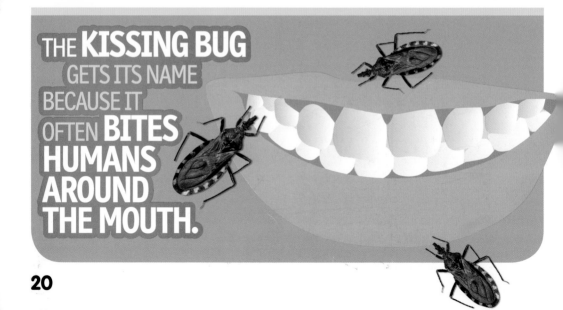

THE **KISSING BUG** GETS ITS NAME BECAUSE IT OFTEN **BITES HUMANS AROUND THE MOUTH.**

THE CORPSE FLOWER, WHICH BLOOMS ONCE EVERY FEW YEARS, SMELLS LIKE ROTTING MEAT.

A supercolony of **ARGENTINE ANTS** stretches **3,700** MILES (6,000 KM) across Europe.

SOME SPECIES OF HORNED TOADS CAN SHOOT A THREE-FOOT STREAM (0.9-m) OF BLOOD OUT OF THEIR EYES.

Among the artifacts at the Mütter Museum, in Philadelphia, Pennsylvania, U.S.A., you will find jars of picked human skin and bedbugs extracted from a person's ear.

MOST PEOPLE **TOOT** 6 TO 20 TIMES A DAY.

MARINE IGUANAS
SNEEZE SALT
ONTO THEIR HEADS TO
FORM SMALL WHITE
"WIGS."

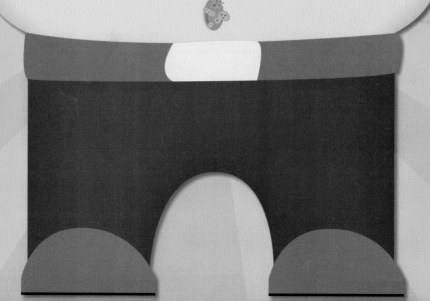

THE AVERAGE **BELLY BUTTON** IS HOME TO **67 DIFFERENT** SPECIES OF **BACTERIA.**

AN ENTOMOLOGIST LET BOTFLY LARVAE LIVE UNDER HIS SKIN FOR TWO MONTHS AND THEN MADE A VIDEO OF THE MAGGOT CRAWLING  **UT.**

THE SURFACE AREA OF YOUR SMALL INTESTINE IS ABOUT THE SIZE OF A TENNIS COURT.

THE BOMBARDIER BEETLE **SQUIRTS A TOXIC,** BOILING-HOT FLUID FROM ITS REAR END.

A DUNG BEETLE CAN MOVE A BALL OF POOP 50 TIMES ITS OWN BODY WEIGHT.

The **tufted titmouse** lines its nest with hair plucked from the tails of **ROADKILL SQUIRRELS.**

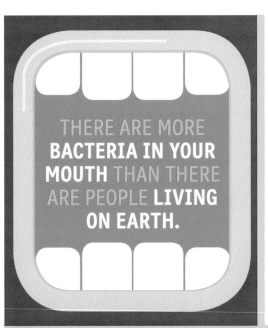

THERE ARE MORE **BACTERIA IN YOUR MOUTH** THAN THERE ARE PEOPLE **LIVING ON EARTH.**

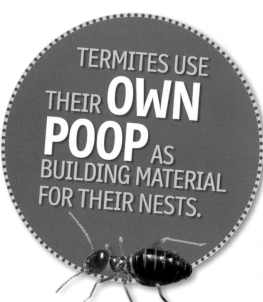

TERMITES USE THEIR **OWN POOP** AS BUILDING MATERIAL FOR THEIR NESTS.

An Italian man once produced a burp lasting **1 minute 13.057 seconds** —the longest belch on record.

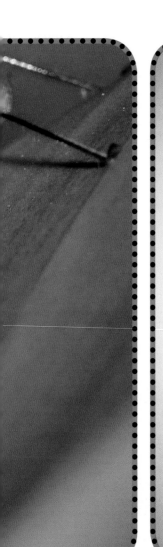

THE ASSASSIN BUG STABS ITS PREY, SUCKS OUT WHAT IT WANTS TO EAT, AND WEARS THE CORPSE ON ITS BACK.

A HANDSHAKE SPREADS 20 TIMES MORE GERMS THAN A FIST BUMP, A STUDY FOUND.

SWEAT HAS NO SCENT. **BACTERIA ON YOUR** SKIN MIX WITH SWEAT AND MAKE IT **STINKY.**

SOME MITES FEAST ON THE OOZE IN RABBITS' EARS.

To deter predators, opossums sometimes DROOL and LIE STIFFLY, trying to look too SICK TO EAT.

COUGH

The **World's** largest **earthworm** is about **three feet** (0.9 m) long and sounds like a draining bathtub when moving through soil.

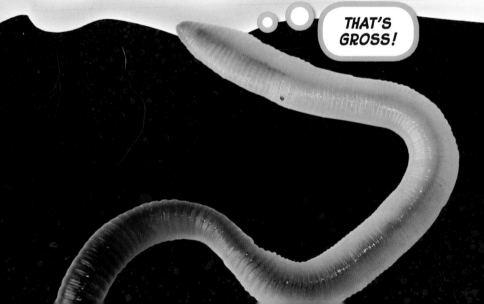

THAT'S GROSS!

ROACHES
SOMETIMES
EAT
HAIR,
SEWAGE,
AND
GLUE.

Your brain is the texture of tofu.

37

Lions cough up hair balls the size of hot dogs.

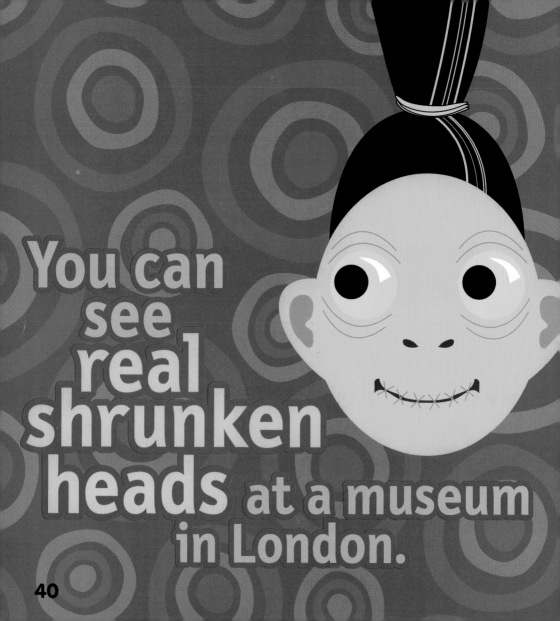

You can see real shrunken heads at a museum in London.

LARVAE

OF THE **NEW WORLD SCREWWORM** HAVE A SPIRAL SHAPE THAT ALLOWS THEM TO **TUNNEL** INTO **FLESH.**

RATS CAN'T

SEWER INSPECTORS
WADE THROUGH RAW SEWAGE AND
dodge rats!
TO FIX CRACKED AND CLOGGED PIPES.

VOMIT.

THERE ARE ABOUT **two million** RATS IN NEW YORK CITY.

The Morbid Anatomy Museum in Brooklyn, New York, U.S.A., once displayed a brooch made of **human teeth.**

THE WORLD'S LARGEST COLLECTION OF **TOENAIL CLIPPINGS CONTAINS** SAMPLES FROM **24,999** PEOPLE.

SOME PEOPLE CAN BELCH OUT BURPS REGISTERING MORE THAN 100 DECIBELS—THAT'S LOUDER THAN A ROARING MOTORCYCLE!

A VENUS FLYTRAP CAN DIGEST A FROG.

AN ASSASSIN SPIDER IMPALES ITS VICTIM, INJECTS IT WITH VENOM, AND LETS IT DANGLE UNTIL IT DIES.

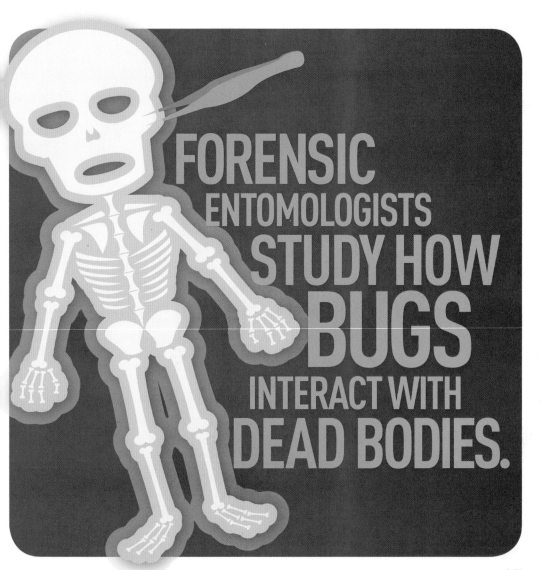

FORENSIC ENTOMOLOGISTS STUDY HOW BUGS INTERACT WITH DEAD BODIES.

ACCORDING TO
ONE IN FIVE ADULTS HAS PEED WHILE

Some **tiny snails** can **survive** being **eaten by birds** –and **are found** alive in their **poop!**

A restaurant owner in England created the "PIE-SCRAPER," a burger that is **5 feet 4 inches** (1.6 m) **tall,** made from more than **18 pounds** (8.5 kg) of meat, and contains **30,000 calories.**

Bacteria can linger on airplane tray tables for three days.

Some red-tinted foods—like candies, yogurt, and ketchup—get their bright hue from the crushed belly of a bug.

In Vietnam, a serving of a **snake's** still-beating heart is considered a delicacy.

In Alaska, U.S.A., you can snack on "ESKIMO ICE CREAM" —a frozen mix of REINDEER FAT, SEAL OIL, GROUND FISH, FRESH BERRIES, and SNOW.

EXCRETIONS FROM A BEAVER'S BEHIND HAVE BEEN USED TO GIVE FOOD

A STRAWBERRY OR RASPBERRY FLAVOR.

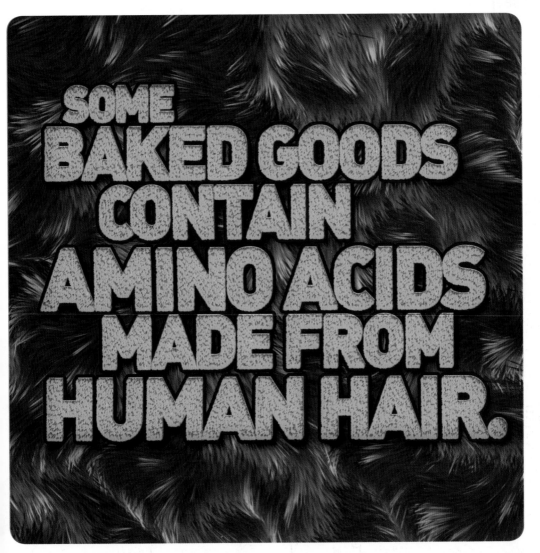

SOME BAKED GOODS CONTAIN AMINO ACIDS MADE FROM HUMAN HAIR.

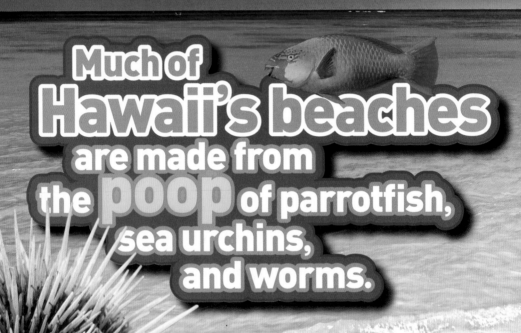

Much of **Hawaii's beaches** are made from the **poop** of parrotfish, sea urchins, and worms.

AT ONE TIME, EUROPEAN ROYALTY TOOK MEDICINE MADE FROM **HUMAN BONES, BLOOD, AND FAT** TO TREAT HEADACHES AND OTHER AILMENTS.

You can eat a **dessert** called **"bloody poop"** out of a **toilet-shaped bowl** at the **Modern Toilet Restaurant** in Kaohsiung, Taiwan.

JELL-O ONCE CAME IN **COFFEE, CELERY,** AND **SEASONED TOMATO FLAVORS.**

Mites live in the hair follicles of your eyelashes.

HÁKARL, A NATIONAL DISH OF ICELAND, IS MADE FROM ROTTEN, FERMENTED SHARK MEAT.

PALEOSCATOLOGISTS=
SCIENTISTS WHO STUDY FOSSILIZED DUNG

One man's **ear hairs** measured **7.1** inches (18 cm) long.

You can find a 40-year-old **Twinkie** at a high school in Maine, U.S.A.—

it's housed in a glass box and is surprisingly mold free!

IN HOT CONDITIONS, A LINEMAN IN FOOTBALL MAY LOSE UP TO **NINE POUNDS** OF SWEAT (4 kg) IN ONE GAME.

A French company sells canned **edible insects,** including cheese-and-bacon-flavored waterbugs, barbecue black scorpions, and **wasabi mealworms.**

AT BUG-THEMED "PESTAURANTS," YOU CAN DINE ON GRASSHOPPER BURGERS, ROASTED CRICKETS, AND ANT LOLLIPOPS.

A man from India once sucked 509 fish through his mouth and snorted them out his nose in one hour.

BASEBALL PLAYER **LUIS GONZALEZ'S** CHEWED BUBBLE GUM ONCE SOLD AT AN AUCTION FOR **$10,000.**

THE SPITBALL, BANNED ALMOST A CENTURY AGO, WAS A BASEBALL COVERED IN SALIVA THAT MADE THE **BALL HARDER TO HIT.**

SCUBA DIVERS IN THE CARIBBEAN GOT CAUGHT IN A 100-FOOT (30-M)-WIDE "**POONADO**" OF WHALE **WASTE**.

BEDBUGS, HEAD LICE, AND FLEAS HAVE BEEN FOUND PRESERVED IN ANCIENT **EGYPTIAN TOMBS.**

A Missouri, U.S.A., barber created a **HAIR BALL WEIGHING 167 POUNDS** (75.7 kg) AND STANDING **FOUR FEET** TALL (1.2 m)

At the World Pigs' Feet Eating Championship in New Jersey, U.S.A., participants competed by eating boiled pigs' parts sprayed with lemon juice.

A typical mattress contains between 100,000 and 10 million dust mites.

A GERMAN MAN SUCKED DOWN 14 OUNCES (396 G) OF KETCHUP THROUGH A STRAW IN JUST 32.37 SECONDS.

IN WISCONSIN, U.S.A., YOU CAN ENTER A "COW CHIP" THROWING COMPETITION WHERE CONTESTANTS FLING DRIED COW POOP.

A British man ate 36 live cockroaches in one minute.

A 19TH-CENTURY ENGLISHMAN NAMED JAMES LUCAS DIDN'T BATHE FOR 25 YEARS.

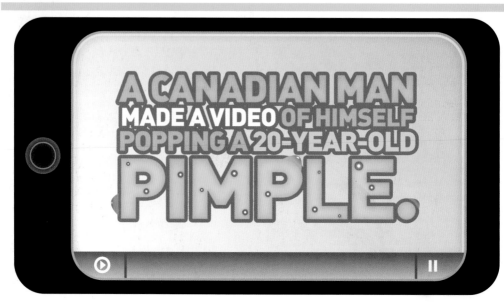

A CANADIAN MAN MADE A VIDEO OF HIMSELF POPPING A 20-YEAR-OLD PIMPLE.

WORMZELS = WORMS TWISTED INTO A PRETZEL SHAPE AND BAKED

A JOCKEY WAS ONCE **HIT IN THE FACE** BY ANOTHER **HORSE'S POOP** DURING A RACE. **HE WON** ANYWAY.

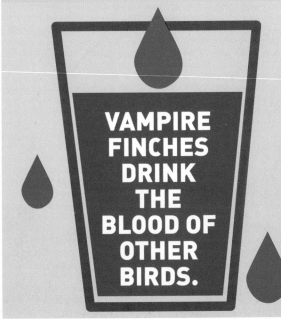

VAMPIRE FINCHES DRINK THE BLOOD OF OTHER BIRDS.

A man in China can **pull a car** by hooking ropes onto **his lower eyelids.**

A woman in Las Vegas, Nevada, U.S.A., has fingernails that are longer than your entire arm.

71

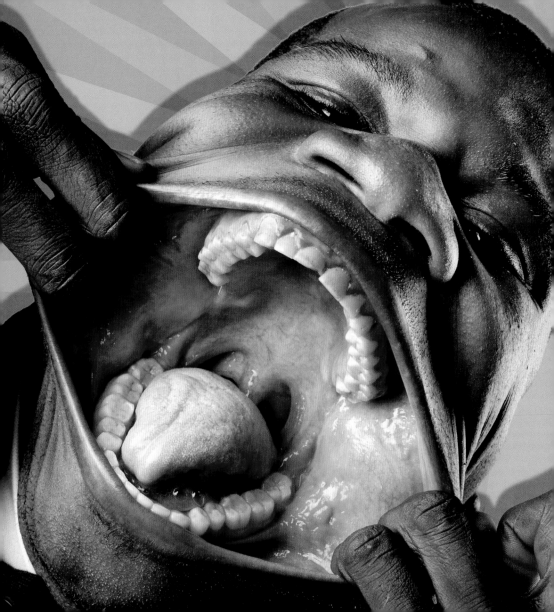

A man nicknamed the "Angolan Jaw of Awe" can open his mouth 6.7 inches— (17 cm) wide enough to cram an entire soda can in sideways.

During the **1500s,** Brits soaked their *fabrics* in *stale urine* to help bind **color dyes** to cloth.

THE BAGS IN **ESTONIAN BAGPIPES,** CALLED TORUPILLS, WERE ORIGINALLY MADE FROM **SEALS' STOMACHS.**

AN **ADULT'S** BLADDER CAN HOLD TWO CUPS OF **URINE.** (473 ML)

In the 1700s, some people believed that the **touch of a dead man's hand** could cure cysts and warts.

Some ancient Romans used *powdered mouse brains* as toothpaste.

Women in ancient Rome dyed their hair with *goat fat and ashes from burned wood.*

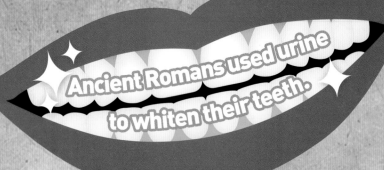

Ancient Romans used urine to whiten their teeth.

In ancient Rome, people socialized at open-air public toilets, some of which could "seat" up to 80 people at a time.

Instead of using toilet paper, ancient Romans would wipe with a shared sponge on a stick.

A man in **China** **once** **stuck** a total of **2,188** needles into his **head** **and** **face.**

A WOMAN IN CHICAGO, ILLINOIS, U.S.A., CAN POP HER EYEBALLS 0.47 INCHES (12 mm) OUT OF HER EYE SOCKETS.

An Australian man **COLLECTED** his belly button lint for **26 YEARS—** and plucked **ENOUGH FLUFF TO FILL THREE JARS.**

For her job as a **FOOT-CARE PRODUCT TESTER,** an Ohio, U.S.A., woman sniffed **5,600 FEET.**

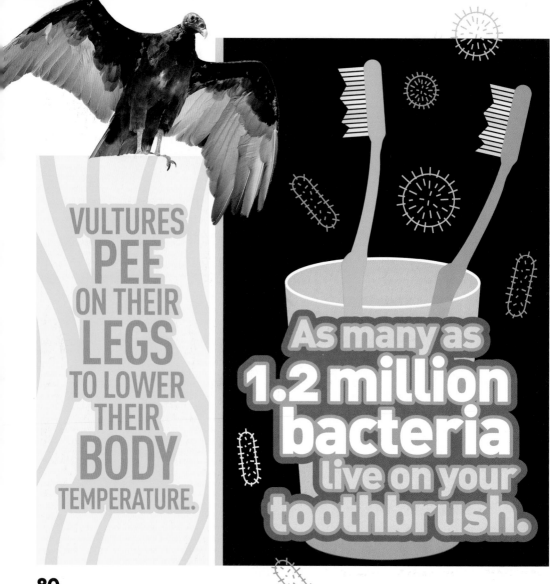

VULTURES **PEE** ON THEIR **LEGS** TO LOWER THEIR **BODY** TEMPERATURE.

As many as **1.2 million bacteria** live on your **toothbrush.**

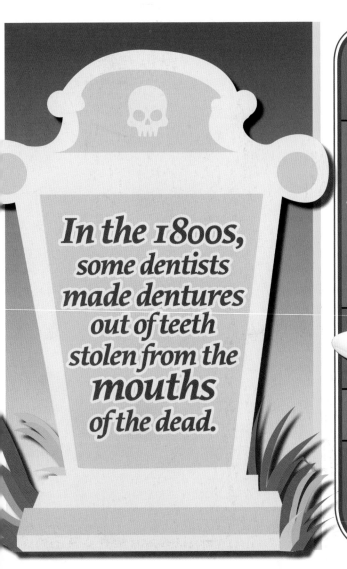

In the 1800s, some dentists made dentures out of teeth stolen from the mouths of the dead.

A SHEEP'S **STOMACH** STUFFED WITH

THE SHEEP'S LIVER, LUNGS, AND HEART, PLUS ONIONS, SPICES, AND OATMEAL

=

HAGGIS, A NATIONAL DISH OF SCOTLAND

A camel's "spit" is partly digested food it burps up and hurls when it feels threatened.

A MOUSE CAN SQUEEZE THROUGH A HLE THE SIZE OF A NICKEL. FOR RATS, THE HOLE NEEDS TO BE THE SIZE OF HALF A QUARTER.

A CLUMP OF CONGEALED COOKING OIL THE **SIZE OF A JUMBO JET** WAS ONCE REMOVED FROM LONDON'S **SEWER SYSTEM.**

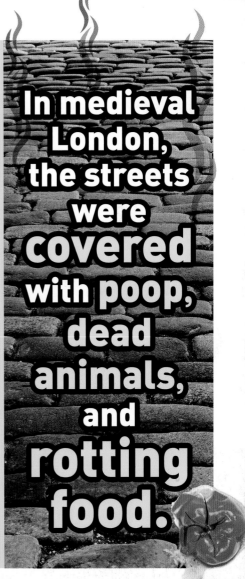

In medieval London, the streets were **covered** with **poop, dead animals,** and **rotting food.**

THE **DECEASED BODY** OF 11TH-CENTURY ENGLISH KING WILLIAM THE CONQUEROR REPORTEDLY **EXPLODED** AS IT WAS BEING STUFFED INTO A **COFFIN.**

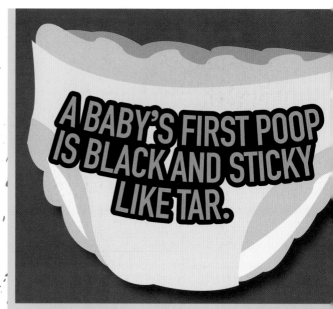

A BABY'S FIRST POOP IS BLACK AND STICKY LIKE TAR.

Many ribbon **worms can regrow** chopped-off body parts **into new worms—** one six-inch (15-cm) worm can turn into **more than 200,000!**

Crocodiles sometimes foam around the eyes when they eat.

A FUNGUS IN THE BRAZILIAN RAIN FOREST INVADES **ANTS' BRAINS** AND **TURNS** THEM INTO **ZOMBIES.**

TERMITES CAN TOOT SO FORCEFULLY THAT THEIR ABDOMENS EXPLODE.

ANCIENT EGYPTIANS TOOK BATHS IN BLOOD, BELIEVING IT WAS GOOD FOR THEIR HEALTH.

Ancient Egyptians tossed their waste into the Nile River—and then used the same water for drinking and bathing.

KING TUT WAS BURIED WITH **145 PAIRS OF** UNDERWEAR.

To fight baldness, ancient Egyptians covered their heads with a mixture of the fat of hippos, crocodiles, snakes, tomcats, and ibexes.

TO MAKE A MUMMY, ANCIENT EGYPTIANS WOULD FIRST PULL THE BRAIN OF THE DECEASED OUT THROUGH THE NOSE.

TICKBIRDS EAT FLIES, MAGGOTS, AND **TICKS** OFF THE HIDES **OF RHINOS.**

91

WHEN YOU GET A SCRAPE IN SPACE, BLOOD DOESN'T RUN DOWN YOUR SKIN—IT FORMS INTO A BLOB OVER THE CUT.

Vampire bats' only food is blood.

93

An engineer invented a machine that turns **POOP INTO** clean drinking **WATER.**

A British man had a **parasitic worm** living in **his brain** for four years.

CHAMPION SPEED EATER MATT STONIE CAN DOWN 62 HOT DOGS—AND BUNS—IN TEN MINUTES!

Thief ants eat kitchen grease and dead rodents.

THAT'S WEIRD!

75 PERCENT of Americans admit to using their phones in the bathroom.

95

DURIAN, A TROPICAL FRUIT FOUND IN SOUTHEAST ASIA, **HAS THE TEXTURE** OF CUSTARD AND **SMELLS LIKE ROTTING GARBAGE.**

A man in Maryland, U.S.A., once plowed snow using a motorized toilet.

AMERICAN CROCODILES THROW UP BITS OF FOOD TO ATTRACT FISH THEY WANT **TO EAT.**

Medieval women used SULFUR to try to burn off their FRECKLES.

April 23 is International Nose Picking Day.

Black pudding, a breakfast staple in England and Ireland, is sausage made from onions, fat, and pigs' blood.

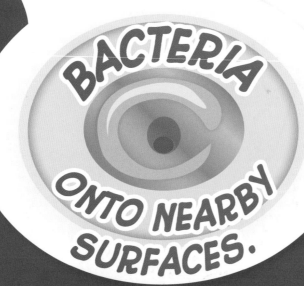

A COMPANY IN BROOKLYN, NEW YORK, U.S.A., SPECIALIZES IN **SCRAPING GUM** OFF CITY SIDEWALKS.

SCIENTISTS FOUND A **1,000-YEAR-OLD MUMMIFIED MONK** INSIDE A STATUE OF A SITTING BUDDHA.

Hippos make their own sunscreen by oozing a thick red substance called "blood sweat."

Sharks **pee through** their skin.

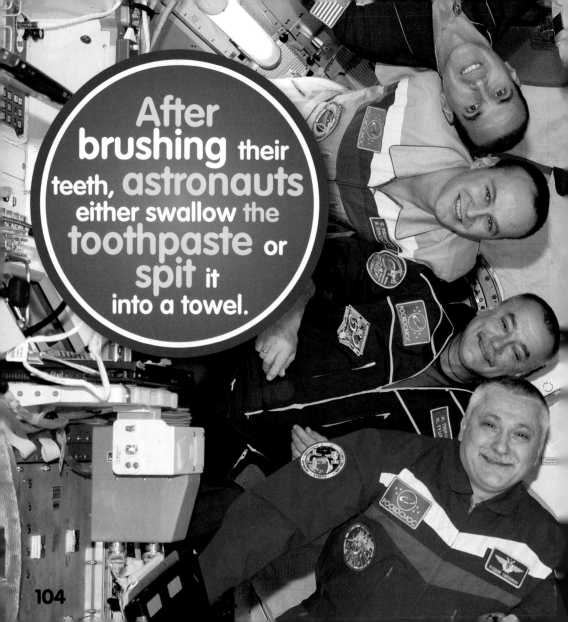

After **brushing** their teeth, **astronauts** either swallow the **toothpaste** or **spit** it into a towel.

Astronauts train in an airsickness-inducing **flight** simulator nicknamed the "vomit comet."

105

TO MAKE THEIR PUPILS LARGER—A MARK OF BEAUTY AT THE TIME—SOME MEDIEVAL ITALIAN WOMEN DROPPED THE JUICE OF THE POISONOUS NIGHTSHADE PLANT INTO THEIR EYES.

A MUSEUM ABOUT THE **PARIS SEWER SYSTEM IS LOCATED** INSIDE THE **PARIS SEWER.**

At a London café, diners eat in booths that used to be urinals.

To stay warm in winter, children in England during the Middle Ages were often **sewn into their clothes**—not changing them for months at a time.

Some ancient soldiers drank the

BLOOD

of the first opponent they killed on the battlefield.

A "VOMIT COLLECTOR" GATHERS PELLETS REGURGITATED BY OWLS AND SELLS THEM FOR STUDENTS TO DISSECT.

An Austrian woman invented a **maggot-breeding home appliance** so people could dine on **protein-rich larvae.**

SCIENTISTS CAN STUDY POLLUTION BY EXAMINING **THE EARWAX** OF BLUE WHALES.

The average home creates **40 pounds** (18 kg) of dust every year.

Dust mites eat the dead

One speck of dust contains **40,000** dust mites.

skin of pets and people.

Monkeys pick **dead skin,** **dirt, and bugs** out of one another's fur.

WHEN DWARF BOAS ARE THREATENED, THEIR EYES FILL WITH BLOOD.

Before toilets were developed, people emptied chamber pots filled with urine out their windows onto city streets.

Ten-inch-long (25-cm) Giant African land snails were found **eating stucco** off the sides of houses in Miami, Florida, U.S.A.

BEDBUGS POOP
BLOOD SPOTS NEAR WHERE THEY HIDE OUT AND FEED.

HIGH LEVELS OF METHANE GAS RELEASED FROM THE **BURPS** AND **TOOTS** OF 90 COWS CAUSED A BARN IN GERMANY TO EXPLODE.

When attacked, sea cucumbers turn their bodies inside out and eject their guts.

Ambergris= the intestinal gunk of **sperm whales** that is used in some **perfumes**

AN AVERAGE ADULT **PEES ENOUGH** EVERY YEAR TO FILL A **150-GALLON** (568-L) HOME AQUARIUM.

SPANISH RIBBED NEWTS **CAN THRUST THEIR RIBS** THROUGH THEIR **SKIN AND** USE THEM AS **WEAPONS.**

Giraffes sometimes use their long tongues to clean their ears and noses.

SLUGS **BREATHE THROUGH** A HOLE **IN THE SIDE** OF THEIR **BODIES.**

ONE OUT OF **TEN BRITISH TRAINS** EMPTIES **TOILET WASTE** RIGHT ONTO THE **RAILWAY TRACKS.**

A MUSEUM IN TURKEY DISPLAYS AN ESTIMATED 16,000 LOCKS OF HAIR LEFT BY ITS VISITORS.

DROPLETS FROM YOUR SNEEZES CAN HANG IN THE AIR FOR 20 MINUTES.

AUSTRALIAN WOMBATS PRODUCE CUBE-SHAPED POOP.

Teenagers **pick their noses** an **average** of **four times** a day.

THAT'S GROSS!

122

43 percent of kids pick off their scabs.

10 PERCENT OF KIDS SAY THEY CHEW ON THEIR TOENAILS!

THAT'S GROSS!

Baby koalas eat **pap**— a soupy substance made from their **mom's poop.**

A TYPE OF **LOUSE** INFESTS A **FISH'S MOUTH, EATS ITS TONGUE,** AND **LIVES THERE** AS THE FISH'S NEW TONGUE.

To help swallow its meal, one species of frog pulls its eyes into the roof of its mouth.

YOUR BODY PRODUCES UP TO 8 CUPS (2 L) OF SPIT A DAY.

Leopard geckos **pee** solid **crystals** instead of liquid urine.

PENGUIN PARENTS REGURGITATE FOOD INTO THEIR BABIES' MOUTHS.

Sloths poop only once a week.

131

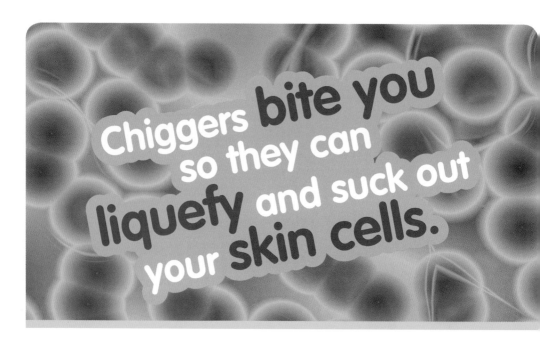

Chiggers **bite you** so they can **liquefy** and **suck out** your **skin cells.**

The air you spew during a

travels **faster than a car** racing down a highway.

Vampire spiders eat **blood-engorged** mosquito **abdomens.**

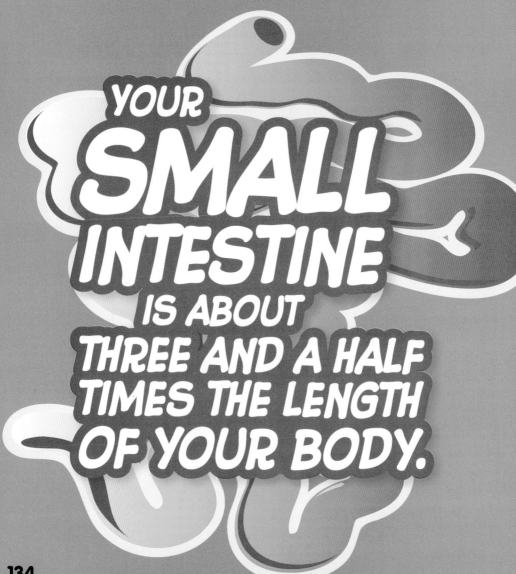

YOUR **SMALL INTESTINE** IS ABOUT THREE AND A HALF TIMES THE LENGTH OF YOUR BODY.

SOME SUGAR IS FILTERED AND BLEACHED WITH CHARRED ANIMAL BONES.

In ancient times, one remedy for treating **blindness** included pouring a mixture of ground pigs' eyes and honey into the ear.

In England, a vial of blood from former British prime minister **Winston Churchill** was put up for auction.

To get rid of a **GUINEA WORM**— A PARASITE that can grow as LONG AS THREE FEET (0.9 m)— you have to wait until IT CRAWLS OUT OF A BLISTER formed ON YOUR SKIN.

Skipper caterpillars can **shoot out poop** pellets as far as **40 times** their body length.

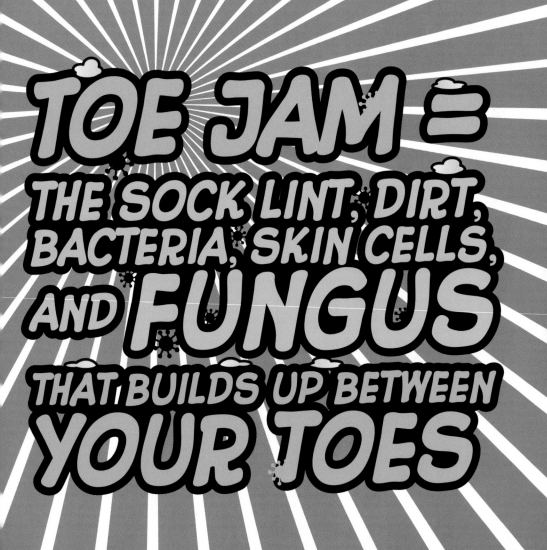

TOE JAM = THE SOCK LINT, DIRT, BACTERIA, SKIN CELLS, AND FUNGUS THAT BUILDS UP BETWEEN YOUR TOES

IN JAPAN, YOU CAN GET A SPA TREATMENT IN WHICH SNAILS CRAWL ACROSS YOUR FACE AND LEAVE TRAILS OF SLIME.

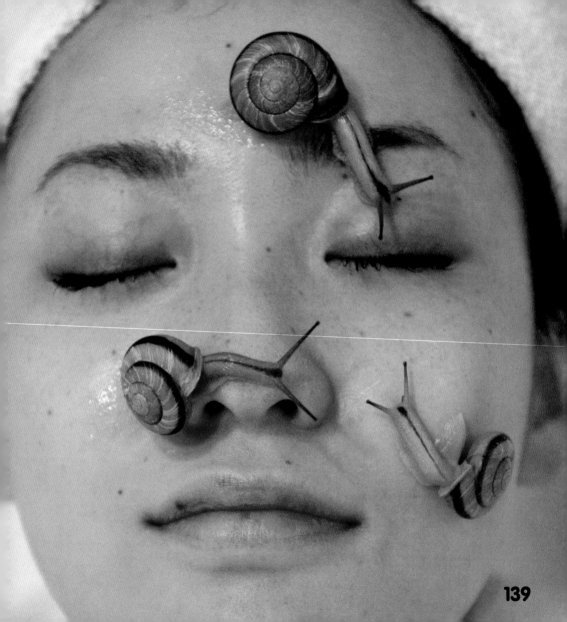

AFTER A FROG SHEDS ITS SKIN, IT EATS IT!

IN THE **1800S,** SOME PEOPLE USED **EARWAX** AS LIP BALM.

One species of turtle pees from its mouth.

THAT'S GROSS!

THE ACID IN YOUR STOMACH CAN DISSOLVE METAL.

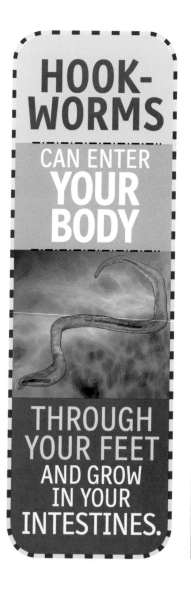

HOOK-WORMS

CAN ENTER **YOUR BODY**

THROUGH YOUR FEET AND GROW IN YOUR INTESTINES.

TURKEY VULTURES CAN **DETECT THE ODOR** OF **ROTTING FLESH** FROM MORE THAN **A MILE AWAY.**
(1.6 km)

Cockroaches can **live** for weeks **without** a **HEAD.**

A TYPE OF BEE FEEDS ON HUMAN TEARS.

A man successfully treated his intestinal disease by ingesting 1,500 parasitic worm eggs.

HAIR GROWS EVERYWHERE ON YOUR BODY

EXCEPT FOR YOUR PALMS, LIPS, EYELIDS, AND THE SOLES OF YOUR FEET.

95 PERCENT OF PEOPLE DON'T WASH THEIR HANDS LONG ENOUGH TO KILL INFECTIOUS GERMS AFTER USING THE TOILET— AND 10 PERCENT DON'T WASH THEIR HANDS AT ALL!

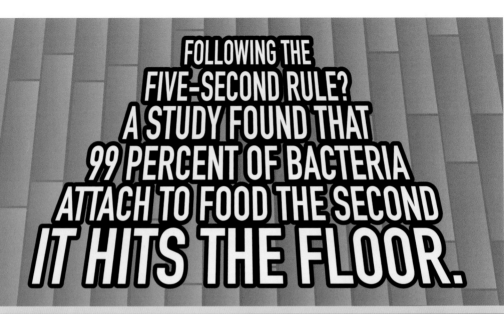

FOLLOWING THE FIVE-SECOND RULE? A STUDY FOUND THAT 99 PERCENT OF BACTERIA ATTACH TO FOOD THE SECOND *IT HITS THE FLOOR.*

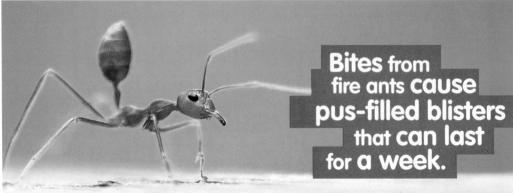

Bites from fire ants **cause** **pus-filled blisters** that **can last** for **a week.**

British scientists discovered **160-MILLION-YEAR-OLD** fossilized reptile vomit.

The same bacterium found in your **sweaty sneakers** is used to ferment **Limburger cheese.**

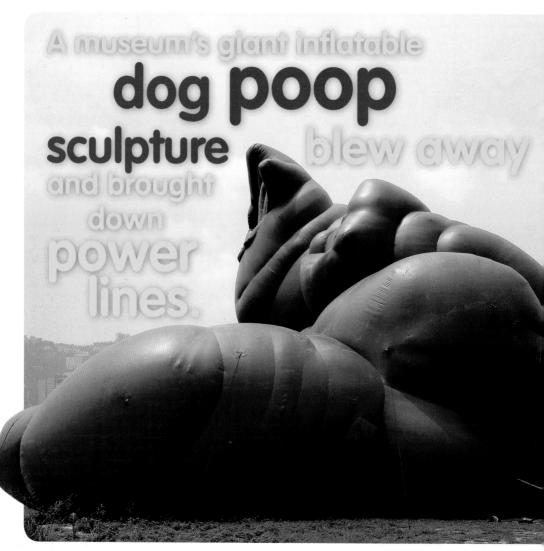

A museum's giant inflatable **dog poop sculpture** blew away and brought down power lines.

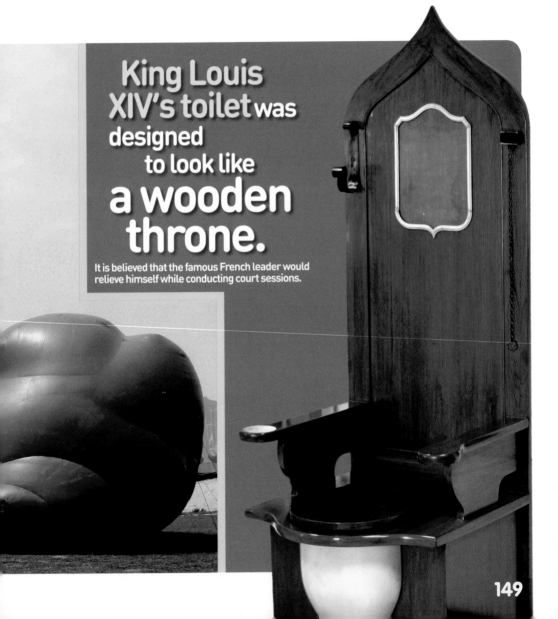

King Louis XIV's toilet was designed to look like a wooden throne.

It is believed that the famous French leader would relieve himself while conducting court sessions.

149

Sea pig =

a type of sea cucumber that feasts on whale carcasses that have fallen to the ocean floor

YUM!

SOME **WOMEN IN ANCIENT EGYPT** USED EYE MAKEUP **MADE FROM** CRUSHED ANT **EGGS.**

A WOMAN IN 17TH-CENTURY FRANCE REPORTEDLY SHED HORNS— INCLUDING ONE 12 INCHES (30 cm) LONG!—FROM HER FOREHEAD.

BATHING WAS ONCE CONSIDERED BAD FOR **YOUR HEALTH.**

BOOGERS ARE THE **DUST, POLLEN, SAND, DIRT, AND OTHER MATERIALS** THAT GET TRAPPED BY YOUR MUCUS.

DURING BATTLES, MEDIEVAL KNIGHTS HAD TO RELIEVE THEIR BLADDERS AND BOWELS INSIDE THEIR ARMOR.

A COMPANY IN WALES MAKES PAPER OUT OF SHEEP POO.

PEACOCKS

THAT'S GROSS!

COOKED IN THEIR **FEATHERS** WERE SERVED AT MEDIEVAL BANQUETS.

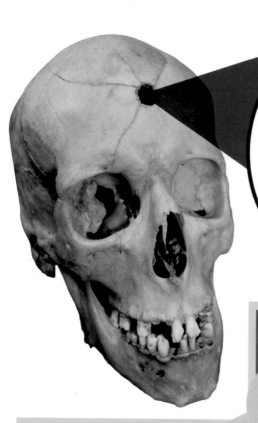

DOCTORS IN ANCIENT PERU DRILLED HOLES IN PATIENTS' SKULLS TO RELIEVE THEIR HEADACHES.

SNAIL SLIME WAS USED AS COUGH SYRUP IN THE MIDDLE AGES.

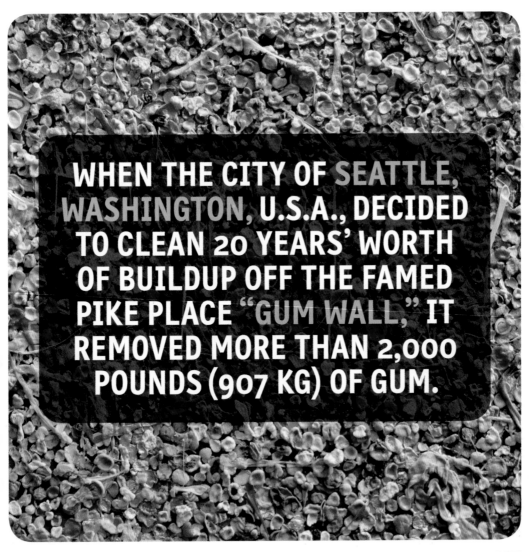

WHEN THE CITY OF SEATTLE, WASHINGTON, U.S.A., DECIDED TO CLEAN 20 YEARS' WORTH OF BUILDUP OFF THE FAMED PIKE PLACE "GUM WALL," IT REMOVED MORE THAN 2,000 POUNDS (907 KG) OF GUM.

A British man found a dead mouse baked into a loaf of bread he was using to make sandwiches.

PEOPLE ONCE **SPREAD COW POOP** ON THEIR **FLOORS TO DISCOURAGE** DISEASE-CARRYING FLEAS.

THAT'S WEIRD!

IT DIDN'T WORK.

Picking your nose in public was acceptable during the Middle Ages.

FRIED GRASSHOPPERS ARE SAID TO TASTE LIKE SPICY POPCORN.

ANCIENT GREEK DOCTOR **HIPPOCRATES** DIAGNOSED HIS PATIENTS BY TASTING THEIR EARWAX AND SMELLING THEIR POOP.

SOME EXPERTS CLAIM THAT THE GIANT WATER BUG TASTES LIKE A JOLLY RANCHER.

AN EYEBALL THE SIZE OF A **SOFTBALL** ONCE WASHED UP ON THE **BEACH** IN FORT LAUDERDALE, FLORIDA, U.S.A.

In the Welsh sport of **bog snorkeling, contestants compete to swim the fastest** through **cold, murky, foul-smelling water.**

U.S. GOVERNMENT REGULATIONS ALLOW UP TO ONE RODENT HAIR IN EVERY 3.5 OUNCES (100 g) OF PEANUT BUTTER SOLD.

THERE MAY BE UP TO **30 FLY EGGS** IN EVERY 3.5 OUNCES (100 G) OF *PIZZA SAUCE.*

LARGE GOBS OF TANGLED WORMS

ONCE FELL FROM THE SKY IN JENNINGS, LOUISIANA, U.S.A.

FISH SCALES ARE SOMETIMES USED TO MAKE SHIMMERY LIPSTICK AND NAIL POLISH.

A WOMAN WON AN ANNUAL "BOOGER SHOOTING CONTEST" BY SENDING HER SNOT ALMOST 20 FEET (6 M) ACROSS A ROOM.

Doctors removed a nine-pound (4.1-kg) **hair ball** from a teenage girl's **stomach.**

A man's **ear canal** became infested with hundreds of **maggots** after a housefly laid eggs in it while he slept.

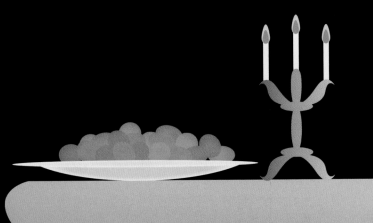

Sweetbreads=
fried glands or organs of cows, pigs, or lambs

ELEPHANT BOOGERS CAN BE AS BIG AS YOUR FIST.

For more than **30 years,** a British man has eaten a diet of **roadkill meat,** whipping up dishes like **fox lasagna and frog leg stir-fry.**

A woman spent 33 days in a room filled with more than 5,000 SCORPIONS.

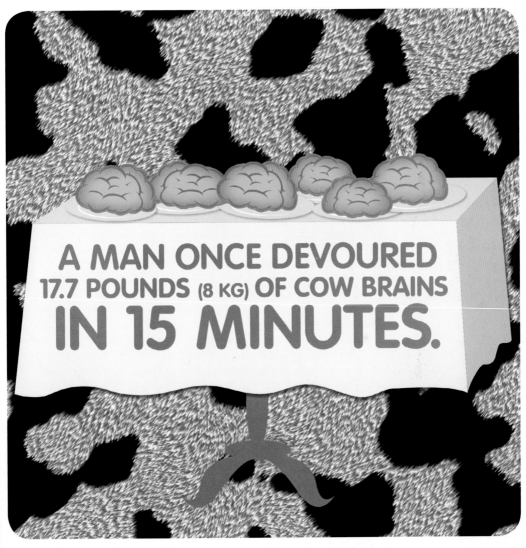

A MAN ONCE DEVOURED 17.7 POUNDS (8 KG) OF COW BRAINS IN 15 MINUTES.

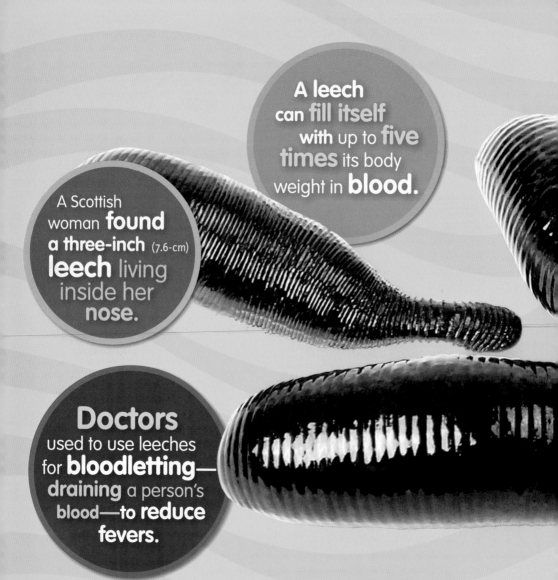

A leech can **fill itself** **with** up to **five times** its body weight in **blood.**

A Scottish woman **found a three-inch** (7.6-cm) **leech** living inside her **nose.**

Doctors used to use leeches for **bloodletting—** **draining** a person's blood—to **reduce** **fevers.**

In the **Middle Ages,** "leech collectors" would wade **in ponds, let leeches** attach to their bare legs, and then **sell them** for **medical** use.

The world's **largest leech** can **grow** to be **as long as** two pencils!

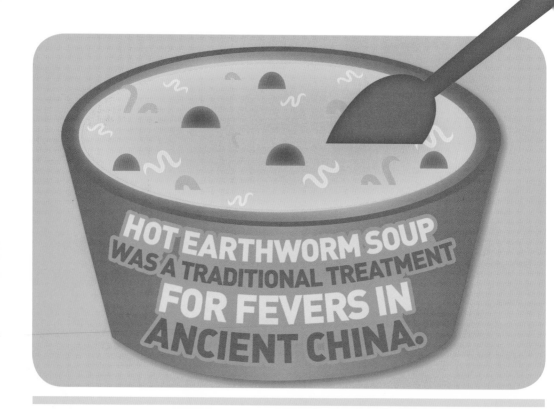

HOT EARTHWORM SOUP WAS A TRADITIONAL TREATMENT FOR FEVERS IN ANCIENT CHINA.

SOME HOSPITALS USE **FLESH-EATING MAGGOTS** TO TREAT INFECTED WOUNDS.

THE ANNUAL **BUG BOWL** COMPETITION IN INDIANA, U.S.A., FEATURES A **CRICKET-SPITTING** CONTEST.

You can see real **human and animal bodies** preserved in

PLASTIC

at the **Plastinarium** in Guben, Germany.

If it weren't for a layer of **sticky mucus** on its walls, **your stomach** would **digest itself.**

THE ENTIRE TOWN OF **ROTORUA, NEW ZEALAND** —KNOWN AS THE **"STINK CAPITAL OF THE WORLD"** —SMELLS LIKE **ROTTEN EGGS.**

A PERFORMANCE ARTIST HAD A THIRD EAR IMPLANTED ON HIS FOREARM.

AN AUSTRALIAN ARTIST MAKES **JEWELRY** OUT OF *HUMAN HAIR, TEETH,* **AND NAIL CLIPPINGS.**

Most of the **dust flecks** you see in a **sunbeam** are shed dead skin.

A CALIFORNIA, U.S.A., MAN MADE A BOLOGNA, CHEESE, AND LETTUCE SANDWICH IN 1 MINUTE 57 SECONDS USING ONLY HIS FEET.

The *Rotten* Sneaker Contest offers cash prizes to kids with the stinkiest shoes.

179

A Canadian man can **DRILL** a **4.5-INCH** (11.4-cm) drill bit into his nose.

CATGUT = A TOUGH CORD MADE FROM ANIMAL INTESTINES USED TO STRING TENNIS RACKETS AND VIOLINS

AN ENGLISH ARTIST CREATED THE "BOGEY BALL" —A MOUND OF DRIED-UP BOOGERS HE SPENT TWO YEARS COLLECTING.

Seal **eyeballs** are **considered a special treat** for **Inuit children** in northern **Canada.**

A COMPANY IS BUILDING HOUSES IN INDONESIA USING BRICKS MADE OF COW DUNG.

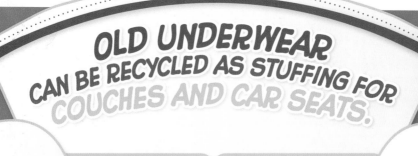

OLD UNDERWEAR
CAN BE RECYCLED AS STUFFING FOR
COUCHES AND CAR SEATS.

A Burmese python once **exploded** after trying to digest an **alligator.**

In the 19th century, a "rat-catcher" earned money by collecting the rodents with his bare hands.

THE **LARGEST ORGANISM** ON EARTH IS THE "**HUMONGOUS FUNGUS.**"

SOME SEA SLUGS **SHOOT TOXIC SNOT** AT THEIR ENEMIES.

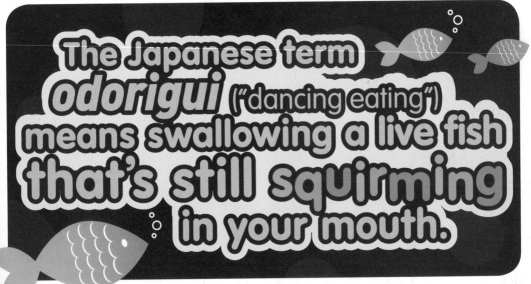

The Japanese term *odorigui* ("dancing eating") means swallowing a live fish that's still squirming in your mouth.

A COMPANY SELLS

SCORPION LOLLIPOPS

IN FLAVORS SUCH AS
BANANA, BLUEBERRY, AND APPLE.

ASTRONAUTS HAVE LEFT NEARLY 100 BAGS OF POOP, URINE, AND VOMIT ON THE SURFACE OF THE **MOON.**

In some parts of China, people eat **monkey brains** with a side of pickled ginger and fried peanuts.

BURGERS MADE OF CRUSHED **FLIES** ARE POPULAR IN LAKE VICTORIA, AFRICA.

A performer nicknamed **Mr. Methane** can toot to the tune of the British national anthem.

A MAN HAD 13 POUNDS [6 KG] OF WARTS SURGICALLY REMOVED FROM HIS BODY.

In 1889, an inventor patented **a locket** you could use to stash your used **chewing gum.**

YOU CAN BRUSH YOUR TEETH WITH TOOTHPASTE FLAVORED LIKE

CURRY.

AT THANKSGIVING, ONE COMPANY SELLS A LIMITED-EDITION SODA FLAVORED LIKE TURKEY AND GRAVY.

Natto = a fermented soybean dish said to smell like sweaty socks

ONE CANDY COMPANY SELLS BACON-FLAVORED GUMBALLS.

An Italian fashion designer made dresses out of **deli meats.**

A STUDENT IN ENGLAND SOAKED IN A **BATHTUB** FULL OF COLD BAKED BEANS FOR TWO HOURS.

A MAN ONCE **BURIED HIMSELF** IN **MORE THAN 10,000**

EARTHWORMS AND THEN **ATE SOME OF THEM** TO BREAK FREE.

A designer invented a lamp that runs on

human blood.

Doctors once discovered a plant growing in a four-year-old boy's nose.

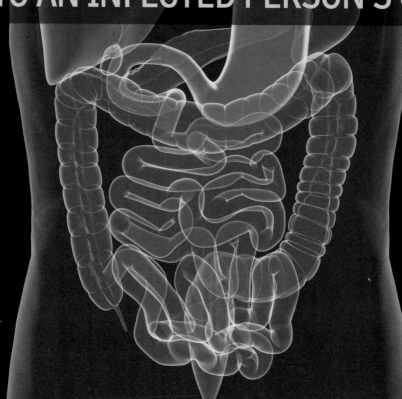

DOCTORS CAN **CURE INTESTINAL** INFECTIONS BY **TRANSPLANTING** **A HEALTHY PERSON'S POOP** INTO AN INFECTED PERSON'S GUT.

AN AMERICAN LONG-DISTANCE RUNNER HAD HIS TOENAILS PERMANENTLY REMOVED.

196

THOUSANDS of RATS

run amok inside the **Karni Mata Temple** in India.

(It's considered good luck if one scampers across your toes!)

Some Japanese ice-cream shops offer novelty flavors such as **slow-boiled egg** and **cow tongue.**

A CANADIAN ARTIST USES **CHEWED GUM** TO MAKE **PORTRAITS** OF **CELEBRITIES.**

25% OF BOTTLED WATER IS JUST TAP WATER.

FOR $425, YOU CAN BUY A PILL THAT WILL MAKE YOUR POOP SPARKLY GOLD.

FACT**FINDER**

Boldface indicates illustrations.

A

Airplane tray tables 51, **51**
Ambergris 116
"Angolan Jaw of Awe" **72–73**, 73
Antifreeze 155, **155**
Ants
    bites from 146, **146**
    colony size 21, **21**
    thief ants 95, **95**
    zombie ants 86, **86**
Argentine ants 21, **21**
Armor 152
Assassin bugs **32–33**, 33
Assassin spiders 46, **46**
Astronauts 92, 104–105, **104–105**, 186, **186**

B

Baby poop 84
Bacon-flavored gumballs 190, **190**
Bacteria
    airplane trays 51, **51**
    belly button 26, **26**
    cheese and shoes 147
    floors 146
    mouth 31
    sofas 20
    and sweat 35
    toilets 99, **99**
    toothbrushes 80, **80**
Baked beans 191, **191**
Baked goods 55
Baldness 89
Baseball 64–65, **64–65**
Bathing
    avoiding 68
    in baked beans 191, **191**

in blood 88
    as unhealthy 151
    in waste water 89
Bathroom behavior 95, 145
Bats 93, **93**
Beaches 56, **56**, 162, **162**
Beauty treatments 138, **139**, 151, **151**, 165
Beavers 54, **54**
Bedbugs 22, 114, **114**
Beds 67, **67**
Bees 144, **144**
Belly buttons 26, **26**, 79, **79**
Berry flavoring 54
Bird's nest soup 13, **13**
Black pudding 98, **98**
Bladder 75, **75**
Blindness 135
Blood
    bathing in 88
    in bedbug poop 114
    birds drinking 69
    Churchill's 136
    drinking 108
    in eyes of dwarf boas 113
    horned toads 21
    lamps powered by 192, **192**
    and leeches 172
    sausage made from 98, **98**
    in space 92
    squirting 15
    vampire bats 93, **93**
Blood sweat 101
Bloodletting 172–173
Blue whales 109
Bog snorkeling 163, **163**
"Bogey ball" (boogers) 181, **181**
Bombardier beetles 27
Boogers
    booger shooting contest 166

collection 181, **181**
    contents 151
    elephant 168
Botfly larvae 27
Brains **94**, **171**
    eating 171, 186
    in medicines 160
    parasitic worms in 94
    removal 89
    texture 37
    as toothpaste 76
Bread 158, **158**
Brooch, made of teeth 44
Bubble gum **100**
    auctioned off 64, **64**
    bacon-flavored 190, **190**
    celebrity portraits in 198
    jewelry 188
    removal 100
    wall of 157, **157**
Bug Bowl (competition) 175
Burgers 51, **51**, 63, 187, **187**
Burmese pythons 182, **182**
Burps 31, 44, 82, 115
Burrowing owls **18–19**, 19
Buses 5, **5**

C

Camels 82, **82**
Canada geese 10–11, **10–11**
Cars 70, **70**
Catgut 180
Celebrity portraits, from gum 198
Chamber pots 113, **113**
Chewing gum **100**
    auctioned off 64, **64**
    bacon-flavored 190, **190**
    celebrity portraits in 198
    jewelry 188

200

FACTFINDER

The publisher would like to thank all who worked to make this book come together: Julie Beer and Sarah Wassner Flynn, writers; Jennifer Agresta, project manager; Becky Baines, project editor; Lisa Jewell, photo editor; Michaela Weglinski, special projects assistant, editorial; Rachel Kenny, design production assistant; Callie Bonaccorsy, special projects assistant, design; Grace Hill, managing editor; Alix Inchausti, production editor.

Since 1888, the National Geographic Society has funded more than 12,000 research, exploration, and preservation projects around the world. The Society receives funds from National Geographic Partners, LLC, funded in part by your purchase. A portion of the proceeds from this book supports this vital work.

For more information, visit
www.nationalgeographic.com,
call 1-800-647-5463,
or write to the following address:
National Geographic Partners, LLC
1145 17th Street N.W.
Washington, D.C. 20036-4688 U.S.A.

Visit us online at nationalgeographic.com/books

For librarians and teachers: ngchildrensbooks.org

More for kids from National Geographic:
kids.nationalgeographic.com

For information about special discounts for bulk purchases, please contact National Geographic Books Special Sales: ngspecsales@ngs.org

For rights or permissions inquiries, please contact National Geographic Books Subsidiary Rights: ngbookrights@ngs.org

NATIONAL GEOGRAPHIC and Yellow Border Design are trademarks of the National Geographic Society, used under license.

Paperback ISBN: 978-1-4263-2335-5
Reinforced library binding ISBN: 978-1-4263-2336-2

Printed in the United States of America
15/QGT-RRDML/1

If you're not TOTALLY grossed out by now, you will be!

From dung-eating bugs to bug-eating humans, get ready to cringe, gag, and squirm while reading the most disgustingly awesome, totally true stories in *That's Gross!*

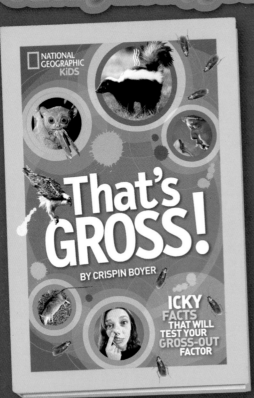

NATIONAL GEOGRAPHIC KiDS

That's GROSS!

BY CRISPIN BOYER

ICKY FACTS THAT WILL TEST YOUR GROSS-OUT FACTOR

Discover MORE fun where THAT came from in the amazing That's series.